ELEPHANTS

ELEPHANTS

JENNY MARKERT

THE CHILD'S WORLD

DESIGN
Bill Foster of Albarella & Associates, Inc.

PHOTO CREDITS
Ralph A. Clevenger: front cover, back cover, 9, 10, 12, 16, 21, 27
Joe Van Os: 2, 6, 15, 18, 23, 28
Robert and Linda Mitchell: 14, 30
Leonard Rue III: 25

Distributed to schools and libraries
in the United States by
ENCYCLOPAEDIA BRITANNICA EDUCATIONAL CORP
310 South Michigan Ave.
Chicago, Illinois 60604

Library of Congress Cataloging-in-Publication Data
Markert, Jenny.
Elephants/Jenny Markert.
p. cm. — (Child's World Wildlife Library)
Summary: Describes the characteristics and behavior
of the elephant.
ISBN 0-89565-724-4
1. Elephants — Juvenile literature.   [1. Elephants.]   I. Title.
II. Series.   91-13380
QL737.P98M369 1991   CIP
599.6'1—dc20   AC

For Mom

On the grassy plains of Africa, peace and quiet are a part of every hot afternoon. Gentle breezes rustle the grasses and tree branches. All around, animals are grazing or resting. In one place, however, noise and action are certain to be found. At the water hole, elephants are taking their afternoon baths.

For elephants, few things feel as good as a bath on a hot afternoon. The water satisfies their thirst and keeps them cool. The massive creatures roll around, splash each other, and bellow with delight. They fill their long trunks with water and spray it over their backs. Older elephants lie down and relax in the water. Younger elephants wrestle and play in it.

After a bath, elephants suck up mud or dirt with their trunks. Then they spray the muck all over themselves. After it dries, the coat of mud protects the elephants' skin from pesky insects and sunburn. So much for being clean!

Elephants are the biggest animals that live on land. Adult elephants weigh about as much as 60 full-grown men. They are nearly as tall as a school bus.

To support their huge bodies, elephants have strong, thick legs. Their legs look a lot like moving tree trunks. Each leg is strong enough to support an elephant's whole body. However, an elephant's legs are not much good for running or jumping. Elephants are normally slow movers. They cannot jump even an inch off the ground!

The two types of elephants — African and Asian — are named for the continents where they live. While most African elephants are wild, many Asian elephants are tame. People train them to lift heavy logs and pull big carts.

One way to tell the two elephants apart is to look at their ears. African elephants have big, floppy ears that cover their necks and shoulders. The ears of Asian elephants are much smaller.

Elephants use their ears for more than just hearing. With their ears held straight out, elephants look even bigger. This helps them frighten away enemies. Their ears are also great fans. On hot days, elephants flap their ears back and forth to keep cool. Flapping ears also make good flyswatters!

Elephants live in family groups, called *herds*, that contain between 10 and 100 elephants. Normally, the elephants in a herd get along well with each other. They are friendly, affectionate, and protective. If one elephant is sick or hurt, the other elephants comfort and protect it. All of the members of an elephant herd help to raise the baby elephants.

Elephant herds do not stay in one place for very long. Instead, they live a nomadic life. They wander through the grasslands in search of water and food. An adult elephant may eat 300 to 600 pounds of food in a single day. That's more than you can eat in an entire year! If elephants stayed in one place very long they would run out of food.

Elephants are strict vegetarians — they eat only plants. They like to munch on tree leaves, bark, and roots. Elephants also eat flowers, bushes, and shrubs. They need so much food to get full that it's hard to be picky!

When elephants eat, they grab food with their long trunks. The trunk is made of muscle and is strong and flexible. The trunk acts like a hand, but it is actually a nose. How would you like to have a nose that hung all the way to the ground?

Elephants have many uses for their long noses. They can use them like a straw, so they can drink water without bending over. An elephant's trunk can also smell a person from two miles away or smell water beneath the ground. It can even lift, pet, or spank a baby elephant. A trunk can also be used like a snorkel when an elephant goes for a swim.

Elephants use their trunks to communicate, too. They grunt and snort through their noses to talk to their friends. If an elephant senses danger, it bangs its trunk on the ground to warn the other elephants. Elephants also can scare away enemies with their trunks. They raise their trunks above their heads and trumpet loudly. This warns the intruder to stay away.

Not many animals are brave enough to attack a herd of elephants. Packs of wild dogs, lions, or hyenas will occasionally attempt a group attack, but they rarely succeed. The strong adult elephants form a protective circle around the weaker members of the herd.

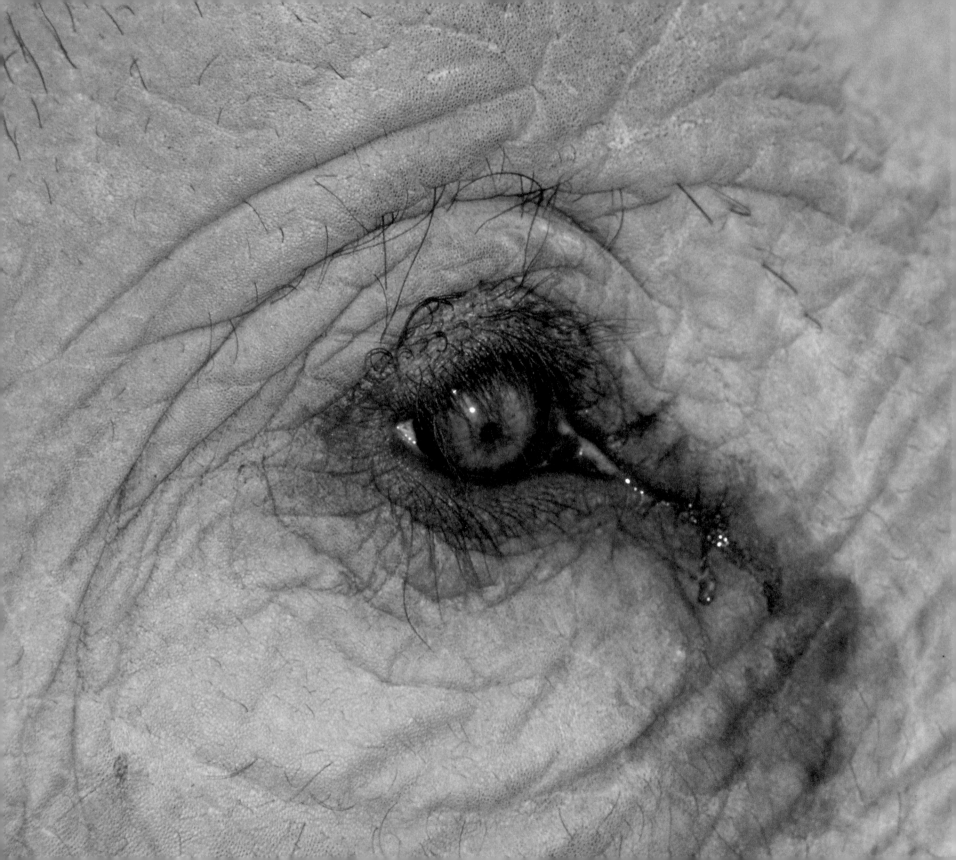

Unfortunately, the elephant's size does not frighten away human beings. Armed with powerful guns, hunters kill thousands of elephants each year. They kill the elephants for their long front teeth, called *tusks*. The tusks are made of ivory, an expensive material that is used to make such things as jewelry, art, and piano keys. Hunters can sell the tusks for thousands of dollars.

Because of the threat from humans, there are fewer elephants each year. If the hunting continues, wild elephants may disappear completely. Luckily, more and more people are realizing that ivory is not as valuable as the survival of the elephant. Now there are strict laws against killing elephants. In addition, many people are refusing to buy ivory or support ivory sellers. Hopefully, this will reduce the demand for ivory and hunters will stop killing elephants.